LEARN PYTHON PROGRAMMING FOR BEGINNERS:

A Beginner's Guide to Comprehending Python. Develop Your Programming Skills and Learn All the Tricks with This Crash Course.

WILLARD D. SANDERS

WILLARD D. SANDERS

© **Copyright 2020 - All rights reserved.**

The content contained within this book may not be reproduced, duplicated or transmitted without direct written permission from the author or the publisher. Under no circumstances will any blame or legal responsibility be held against the publisher, or author, for any damages, reparation, or monetary loss due to the information contained within this book. Either directly or indirectly.

Legal Notice: This book is copyright protected. This book is only for personal use. You cannot amend, distribute, sell, use, quote or paraphrase any part, or the content within this book, without the consent of the author or publisher.

Disclaimer Notice: Please note the information contained within this document is for educational and entertainment purposes only. All effort has been executed to present accurate, up to date, and reliable, complete information. No warranties of any kind are declared or implied. Readers acknowledge that the author is not engaging in the rendering of legal, financial, medical or professional advice. The content within this book has been derived from various sources. Please consult a licensed professional before attempting any techniques outlined in this book.

By reading this document, the reader agrees that under no circumstances is the author responsible for any losses, direct or indirect, which are incurred as a result of the use of information contained within this document, including, but not limited to, errors, omissions, or inaccuracies.

WILLARD D. SANDERS

TABLE OF CONTENTS

INTRODUCTION **8**
CHAPTER 1: WHAT IS PYTHON **10**
    WHAT IS PYTHON? 10
    HISTORY AND EVOLUTION 11
    DIFFERENCE BETWEEN PYTHON 2 VS PYTHON 3 15
CHAPTER 2: ADVANTAGES AND DISADVANTAGES **18**
    ADVANTAGES OF PYTHON LANGUAGE 18
        It is Easy to Work with *18*
        It Has Lots of Power *19*
        Many Libraries to Work With *20*
        Easy to Read *20*
        It is an OOP Language *21*
CHAPTER 3: PYTHON INSTALLATION **24**
    INSTALL PYTHON ON LINUX 24
        Package-Managed Installation *24*
        Debian-based, like Ubuntu *25*
    INSTALL PYTHON ON WINDOWS 27
    INSTALL PYTHON ON MAC 28
CHAPTER 4: LEARNING PYTHON FROM SCRATCH **32**
    DATA TYPES 32
        Numbers *32*
        Lists in Python *38*
    STRING IN PYTHON 58
        Accessing items in a string *60*
        Deleting or Changing in Python *61*
        String Operations *61*
        String Iteration *62*
        Membership Test in String *62*
        String Formatting in Python *63*
        Escape Sequences in Python *63*
    WORKING WITH FILES 64
        Reading from a File *67*
        File Pointer *68*

- *File Access Modes* 72
- *Writing to a File* 74
- *Practice Exercise* 75
- PYTHON TUPLES 77
  - *Example* 81
  - *Negative Indexing* 82
  - *Slicing* 83
  - *Available Tuple Methods in Python* 84
  - *Exercise* 86
  - *Exercise* 86
  - *Exercise* 87
  - *Exercise* 87
- PYTHON SETS 88
  - *Exercise* 92
  - *Exercise* 93
  - *Exercise* 94
- FUNCTIONS 94
  - *Understanding Functions Better* 95
  - *def say_hi():* 96
  - *Output:* 97
  - *Return Statement* 99
  - *return number number number* 100
  - *Random function in Python* 101

CHAPTER 5: OPERATION IN PYTHON 102

- THE PYTHON OPERATORS 102
  - *Arithmetic Operators* 103
  - *Comparison Operators* 105
  - *Logical Operators* 106
  - *Assignment Operators* 107

CHAPTER 6: CLASSES 110

- DEFINITION OF A CLASS 110
  - *Classes and Objects in Python* 112
  - *Syntax* 113
  - *Class or Object Instantiation* 113
  - *Data Encapsulation/Data Hiding* 114
  - *Polymorphism* 116
  - *Creating an Object in Python* 117
  - *Constructors* 118

- *Deleting Objects and Attributes* *119*
- *Deleting an Object* *119*
- *Inheritance in Python* *120*
- *Operator + Overloading* *123*
- DICTIONARIES 126
  - *Clear method* *128*
  - *Get method* *128*
  - *From keys* *128*
  - *Keys* *128*
  - *Pop* *128*
  - *Exercise* *129*
  - *Exercise* *130*
  - *Exercise* *130*
  - *Exercise* *132*
- HANDLING YOUR EXCEPTIONS 133
  - *How to Raise an Exception* *134*
  - *How to Define My Exceptions* *138*

CONCLUSION 142

WILLARD D. SANDERS

INTRODUCTION

The following chapters of this book will discuss Python as a programming language. Each chapter will take you on an in-depth journey into understanding the Python programming language. This book was written to provide the reader with an understanding of Python. The author of this book has conducted thorough research through sources believed to be reliable to come up with the relevant information on the topic.

Go ahead and read through the entire book, get the knowledge, and be informed about the key things that you need to know about this particular topic. Python is a programming language that is often recommended for beginners to try messing up things and falling in love with programming. One of the major reasons for the widespread popularity of Python is its simplicity and the power of making things done with less code. Even after the entrance of tens of programming languages in the past decade python doesn't lose its charm and we are pretty confident that it is going to stay.

This book is primarily for people who are relatively new to programming and, more specifically, those who want to discover the world of Python. This book will take you through the fundamentals of programming and Python.

WILLARD D. SANDERS

CHAPTER 1:

WHAT IS PYTHON

What is Python?

Python is an awesome decision on machine learning for a few reasons. Most importantly, it's a basic dialect at first glance. Regardless of whether you're not acquainted with Python, getting up to speed is snappy if you at any point have utilized some other dialect with C-like grammar.

Second, Python has an incredible network that results in great documentation and inviting and extensive answers in StackOverflow (central!).

Third, coming from the colossal network, there are a lot of valuable libraries for Python (both as "batteries included" an outsider), which take care of essentially any issue that you can have (counting machine learning).

However, here's the caveat: libraries can and do offload the costly computations to the substantially more performant (yet much harder to use) C and C++ are prime examples. There's NumPy, which is a library for numerical calculation. It is composed of C, and it's quick. Therefore, each library out there that includes serious estimations utilizes it—every one of the libraries recorded next utilizes it in some shape. On the off chance that you read NumPy, think quickly.

In this way, you can influence your computer scripts to run essentially as quickly as handwriting them out in a lower level dialect. So, there's truly nothing to stress over with regards to speed and agility.

Python is one of the most important programming languages nowadays, being a general-purpose language.

With this language, you can create a huge and varied amount of applications, because it allows you to create different kinds of applications since it doesn't have a defined purpose.

History and Evolution

Since computers were first invented, many people have had the job to make them more useful. To make this happen, there are a ton of programming tools that have been developed over the years to turn the instructions the computer is given into code that the computer can execute. When this first started, assembly language was the main type. While it did allow you to create programming that was tailored and then optimized for the low memory systems of that time, it was hard to learn, read, and maintain and only a few people could use it.

As computer technology grew and many systems became more complex, the programming languages needed to change as well. Some higher-level languages including Lisp, Cobol, and Fortran were produced to produce punch cards which the computers were able to read and then execute the instructions that were found on the card. Programming with this kind of tool was a lot easier than the languages in the past, allowing more people to write the complex programs they needed.

As time started to go on, there were a lot of improvements that were made to some of the technology that we are working with now, and it has resulted in a lot of better storage methods when it comes to our programs and more. For example, some of those punch cards have been replaced with a type of magnetic tape, and then it was all moved over to work with a disc drive. As these new inventions came out, the tools to work on these programs improved as well.

Basic was one of the first coding languages that was designed to be easy to read through and this one was developed in the 1960s. Then in the 1970s, we saw the introduction of Pascal and C, and these became tools that helped us to get a really simple and structured kind of programming language that would help a programmer to get the efficient code that they want. You will find that the structured languages like these would not have to rely on the go-to statement found in some of the other languages. Instead, these programs would rely on a flow that has features including conditional statements, functions, and loops like we will talk about later in this guidebook. These features were nice because they would allow a new programmer to make their applications with the help of standalone reusable routines, which would then be able to lower the amount of time that it would take to develop the program, and even debug it so that the program would work the way that you would like.

It was in the 1980s when the next big advancement in programming happened This was where C++, and a few other languages, turned into OOP languages, or object-oriented programming languages. There are a number of these that are now available and usable, but they were useful because they helped us to hold onto our information better. While these tools of OOP languages were powerful and had some new capabilities when it came to coding, many times they would be seen as special because they could cut out some of the challenges that came with coding.

As the use and the popularity of computers started to grow, and it became common for more people to use them, it was also an important factor to have a language for programming that was easy to use, one that we can use on a lot of different platforms. Because of this need, the language that we know as Python today was developed.

Python is going to be a general-purpose programming language. Whether you are a beginner or someone who has been in the coding world for some time, you will find that this language is easy to learn while still making sure that there is a lot of power behind it to get those codes done. You can use this for a lot of different purposes, from some general housekeeping tasks for your system to just having fun and making your programs and games. Of course, when you compare this language to some of the others out there, you will also notice that Python is going to have a lot of rules and structures that you must follow to get this to work. No matter what codes you would like to write in Python, you will need to follow the rules and ensure that the compiler is ready to handle it all. The good news is that the rules are pretty simple with this language and you will find that this language is simple, powerful, and compact all in one. As a beginner, it is easier to catch onto this kind of coding language than you think, and before long, and with the help of this guidebook, you will be able to get everything to work the way you would like and will be writing your codes in no time.

In the past, a lot of people were worried about learning a coding language. They worried that these languages were too tough to learn, that they would just get frustrated, and that only those who had spent their whole lives around computers could even attempt to write their codes. And maybe with some of the older codes, this was true. Thanks to a lot of the newer codes that have been introduced recently, the idea that only those gifted in computer programming could code has faded away. With many of the codes that are coming out now, including Python, anyone can learn a few of the syntaxes for what they want to do, or even find some premade codes online and make some changes. And since many of these codes are open-sourced, it is easier than ever to learn how to use them and develop the codes to meet your needs. You will find that many of the modern languages that are used for coding are going to be a lot better and easier to use than what we were able to find in the past with most coding languages. Gone are the days that even professionals would run into troubles regularly when it was time to find the bugs in the system. Now anyone and everyone can learn how to use this coding language for these needs. And this is mainly because we have a lot of great OOP languages to work within Python.

Difference between Python 2 vs Python 3

There are many coding languages out there that you can use. Some of them are pretty basic to learn, and some have a bit more power behind them. Many people have at least interacted with Java or JavaScript when they go to a website, especially one that has a pop-up of any kind. If you have worked with a Windows computer, you may have experimented with some of the languages that are found there. Or maybe you are coming to this guidebook as a completely new beginner to all things coding and you want to know where to start.

The options can seem pretty overwhelming when you start. All the many languages are going to follow their own rules on how to write the codes and what you can do with the code as well. But if you are looking for a coding language that has a ton of power for a beginner, one that can easily stop and avoid others, one that offers you many choices and allows you to implement it with many other coding languages at the same time, then Python is the right choice for you.

Beginners and more advanced coders alike love working with the Python coding language. There are many benefits, but the primary part is that it was developed with the beginner in mind. In the last few decades, there has been a push in much of the world of technology to start making it easier to get more people to come in and join the fun. They see that there are benefits to inviting more people. More games can be created, more bugs fixed in programs, and just more innovation compared to the times when only a few people even had any idea how to code in the first place.

In this guidebook, we are going to spend some time exploring the world of Python, looking at what this coding language is all about, and helping you to write some of your codes by the time that you are done. Don't be scared about this coding language. While there are a lot of people who may be intimidated when they hear about coding because they worry it will be too hard, you will quickly see a ton of examples of how Python works. Then you will be ready to dive right in and see what your creativity and hard work can do.

WILLARD D. SANDERS

CHAPTER 2:

ADVANTAGES AND DISADVANTAGES

Advantages of python language

It is Easy to Work with

The first benefit that most people are going to enjoy when it comes to using the Python language is that it is very easy to use. This language was designed for use with a beginner, and the whole purpose is to make sure that anyone, even those who may not be well-versed in doing any kind of programming at all, will be able to learn and write some of the codes of their own that they would like. This language is meant to help a beginner, someone who has never had a chance to work with coding in the past, learn how to do some of this coding, and get the results that they would like. There are also a lot of different things that you can do when you work with the Python coding language. It is designed to help with almost any kind of coding that you are interested in handling, from some of the basics of writing your projects to help out with data analysis and machine learning if you so choose. There is just so much that you can do with this kind of language and many people are jumping on board to learn how to work all of these different angles with ease thanks to the Python coding language.

It Has Lots of Power

Even though this is a coding language that is meant to help us out with some of the basics of coding, you will find that there is quite a bit of strength and power behind what we can do with it. Even more advanced problems can be easily handled when we are looking at this kind of language, and you will find that with the added extensions and libraries that are available with Python, it is easy to figure out how to write codes that work with some complex coding and programming problems Some people hear about how easy it is to work with Python and they worry that there is not going to be enough strength and power behind it to get started. They think they need to go with another option because this one will not have the strength of the features that are needed to get things done. But, once you mess around with some of the codes that we will do with this language, you will find that it is going to have plenty of power and a ton of the features that you need to get anything done.

Many Libraries to Work With

While we are at it, you will find that a lot of the libraries and extensions that come with the Python language are going to be great as well. You can already do a lot of work with the standard Python language, but you will also find that there are additional libraries that work well with Python and can help us to expand out what we can do with programming in this language. From libraries that can help us out with math, science, machine learning, data science, and more, you will find that the Python coding language is one of the best options for you to work with. From here, we will also find that the Python language is going to be one that can work well with others. For some of the basics that we will discuss in this guidebook, this is not going to seem like that big of a deal. But when we get into some things like machine learning and data science with this language, the fact that we can combine Python with other languages is going to help us get more done.

Easy to Read

We will also see that the Python coding language is going to be a great option to work with when you want to make sure that things stay organized and easy to read through. There are a lot of other coding languages out there that you can choose from, but that does not mean that they are the right ones for you. In most cases, beginners are going to find that working with an OOP language, just like Python is, is one of the best ways to keep the information organized and easy to use.

It is an OOP Language

The fact that Python is an OOP language is going to be good news for you. We will explore this a bit more in the next few chapters, but this basically means that the code is split up into classes, and then the objects that show up in the code will fit into one of these classes. This is the best way to make the code as efficient as possible and will ensure that you can bring up the right parts, at the right times so that your code will work the way that you want.

Disadvantages of Python language

Since it is an interpreted language it has been observed that it is often slower in execution than other languages.

Python is not compatible with many browsers and mobile computing.

Since the typing is dynamic therefore it requires more testing as the errors show up only during run time.

Now that we know about the pros and cons of Python, let us see in comparison with a few popular languages as to how Python stands out amongst them.

Python has been often compared to languages such as JavaScript, Java, Perl, Smalltalk, Tcl, and C++. These comparisons can be enlightening to know the nuances of this language. However, in a practical environment, the choice of a programming language is typically dictated by terms such as availability, training, prior investment, and of course the cost involved. Let us look at some comparisons which we have drawn with other languages:

Java—The programs run under Python are 3-5 times shorter than Java programs. This is due to the high level and dynamic typing of the language. The syntactic support is built directly into the language. For example, if you want to print "hello world" in Python one simply has to type: **print ('hello world')** whereas in Java the same command would be covered in 4 lines. Java Script-Unlike JavaScript, Python supports the writing of large programs with better codes by using object-oriented programming *Perl*- Both languages have a different philosophy where Perl supports common application-oriented tasks such as report generation, file scanning, etc., whereas Python supports common programming methods such as designing a data structure. It encourages programmers to write readable and maintainable codes.

Tcl—As compared to Python, Tcl is weak on data structures and executes codes which are much slower. It also lacks the feature of writing large scale programs.

Smalltalk—The standard library of Smalltalk is more defined whereas in the case of Python it has more facilities for dealing with the World Wide Web realities such as email, FTP, and HTML.

C++- Just like Java when compared to C++ the programming code is 5-10 times shorter. It is said that a C++ programmer can finish in a year Python programmer can finish in two months.

CHAPTER 3:

PYTHON INSTALLATION

Install Python on Linux

There are two ways to install Python on a Linux system – source installation or package-managed installation. While the latter is preferable, we will discuss both methods:

Package-Managed Installation

The most common method of installing Python on Linux is to use the Linux package systems. This also ensures that you can easily upgrade Python when the time comes. Depending on which distribution of Linux you are using, you will need to use one of these commands:

Debian-based, like Ubuntu

apt-get install python

RPM-based, like Red Hat or Fedora:

urpmi python

Gentoo:

emerge python

If you don't see the latest version of the installation, you will need to manually install Python, which we will talk about shortly.

You will need to install some extra packages if you want a full installation – these are optional but recommended if you want to be able to profile your programs or have code C extensions. To make sure you have a full installation, install these packages by typing them in at the command prompt:

- *python-dev* – has Python headers for use in compiling C modules

- *python-profiler* – has non-GPL modules for use on Debian, Ubuntu, and other full GPL Linux distributions

- *gcc* – used for compiling extensions that have C code in them

Compiling Sources

To do a manual installation, you need to use the cmmi process:

- Configure

- Make

- Make Install

This process will perform a Python compilation and then install it on your system.

To get the latest archive for Python, go to http://python.org.download

To perform the download, we use wget with MacPorts or apt – see www.gnu.org/software/wget for more information on your specific distribution.

To build Python, we are going to use gcc and make. Make is a program we use to read Makefile configuration files and make sure that all of the requirements are met to compile Python. It is also used as a way of driving the installation and it is invoked using the make and configure commands. gcc is better known as the GNU C Compiler and it is an open-source compiler that is used a lot in building programs. Ensure that both of these have been installed on your Linux system.

To build Python and install it, type in this command at the command prompt:

cd /tmp

wget http://python.org/ftp/python/2.5.1/Python2.5.1.tgz

tar -xzvf tar -xzvf Python2.5.1.tgz

cd Python2.5.1

./configure

make

sudo make install

This also installs all the headers for binary installations that are normally found in python-dev. Once all of this is installed, you should be able to reach Python from the Linux shell.

Install Python on Windows

We can install Python on a Windows system in the same way as a Linux, but this is an incredibly painful way of doing it. Instead, go to http://python.org/downlaod and download the version of Python that you want. All the instructions are provided, making it simple to do. Provided you do not change any of the defaults, you will find Python installed at c:\Python25 and not in the Program Files folder where you would expect to find it. This cuts out the risk of space in the path. Finally, we need to change the PATH environment variable, enabling us to get Python from the DOS shell. To do this:

- Find the icon for My Computer on your version of Windows and right-click on it
- This will open the System Properties dialog box
- Click on the tab for Advanced

- Click on the button for Environment Variables

Edit the PATH system variable to input two new paths, each separated with a semicolon (;). The paths to be added are:

- c:\Python25 – this will enable python.exe to be called

- c:\Python25\Scripts – this will enable installed third scripts to be called Python should now run in the command prompt. To open this, open the Run dialog box, press the Windows key and R at the same time. Type cmd in the box and click on Open. At the prompt type in *c:/>python* If you see a message like the one below, Python is installed:

Python 2.5.2 (#71, Oct 18 2006, 08:34:43) [MSC v.1310 32 bit (Intel)] on

win32

Type "help", "copyright", "credits" or "license" for more information.

>>>

Python is ready to use.

Install Python on Mac

Although the Mac already comes with Python installed, this is likely to be out of date and is only good for learning, not for developing. The best thing is to install a new version of Python and to do that, we need a C compiler.

Go to the Mac App Store and download XCode

Open a terminal and type in xcode-select –install – this will install the command line tools

The next step is a package manager and the best one is called Homebrew and to install this, open a terminal and run the following code:

$ usrbin/ruby -e "$(curl -fsSL https://raw.githubusercontent.com/Homebrew/install/master/install)"

Follow the on-screen instructions to install Homebrew and then prepare to make changes to the PATH environment variable. To do this, add this line at the bottom of the ~/.profile file: *export PATH=usrlocal/bin:usrlocal/sbin:$PATH*

Now you can install Python. For Python 2.7, type this is at the command:

$ brew install python

For Python 3, type this:

$ brew install python3

This will only take a couple of minutes at the most.

Homebrew will also install Pip and Setuptools. Setuptools lets you download and install Python software via a network, normally the Internet, using just a single command – *easy_install.* This will also let you add this capability for network installation to your Python software. Pip is used for the easy installation and management of Python packages and is recommended instead of using *easy_install.*

CHAPTER 4:

LEARNING PYTHON FROM SCRATCH

Data Types

Numbers

Python accommodates floating, integer, and complex numbers. The presence or absence of a decimal point separates integers and floating points. For instance, 4 is an integer while 4.0 is a floating-point number.

On the other hand, complex numbers in Python are denoted as r+tj where j represents the real part and t is the virtual part. In this context, the function type() is used to determine the variable class. The Python function is an instance() invoked to decide which specific class function originates from.

Example

Start IDLE.

Navigate to the File menu and click New Window.

Type the following:

number=6

print(type(number)) #should output class int print(type(6.0)) #should output class float complex_num=7+5j

print(complex_num+5)

print(isinstance(complex_num, complex)) #should output True Important: Integers in Python can be of infinite length. Floating numbers in Python are assumed precise up to fifteen decimal places.

Number Conversion

This segment assumes you have prior basic knowledge of how to manually or using a calculator to convert decimal into binary, octal, and hexadecimal.

Check out the Windows Calculator in Windows 10, Calculator version 10.1804.911.1000 and choose programmer mode to automatically convert.

Programmers often need to convert decimal numbers into octal, hexadecimal, and binary forms. A prefix in Python allows the denotation of these numbers to their corresponding type.

Number System Prefix

Octal '0O' or '0o'

Binary '0B' or '0b'

Hexadecimal '0X or '0x'

Example

print(0b1010101) #Output:85

print(0x7B+0b0101)   #Output: 128   (123+5)   print(0o710) #Output:710

Assignment

Create a program in Python to display the following: i) 0011 11112

ii) 7478

iii) 9316

Type Conversion

Sometimes referred to as coercion, type conversion allows us to change one type of number into another. The preloaded functions such as float(), int() and complex() enable implicit and explicit type conversions.

The same functions can be used to change from strings.

Example

Start IDLE.

Navigate to the File menu and click New Window.

Type the following:

int(5.3) #Gives 5

int(5.9) #Gives 5

The int() will produce a truncation effect when applied to float numbers. It will simply drop the decimal point part without rounding off. For the float() let us take a look: Start IDLE.

Navigate to the File menu and click New Window.

Type the following:

float(6) #Gives 6.0

complex('4+2j') #Gives (4+2j)

Assignment

Apply the int() conversion to the following: a. 4.1

b. 4.7

c. 13.3

d. 13.9

Apply the float() conversion to the following: e. 7

f. 16

g. 19

Decimal in Python
Example

Start IDLE.

Navigate to the File menu and click New Window.

Type the following:

(1.2+2.1)==3.3 #Will return False, why?

Explanation The computer works with finite numbers and fractions cannot be stored in their raw form as they will create an infinitely long binary sequence.

Fractions in Python
The fractions module in Python allows operations on fractional numbers.

Example

Start IDLE.

Navigate to the File menu and click New Window.

Type the following:

Important

Creating my_fraction from float can lead to unusual results due to the misleading representation of binary floating-point.

Mathematics in Python

To carry out mathematical functions, Python offers modules like random and math.

Start IDLE.

Navigate to the File menu and click New Window.

Type the following:

import math

print(math.pi) #output:3.14159....

print(math.cos(math.pi)) #the output will be -1.0

print(math.exp(10)) #the output will be 22026.4....

print(math.log10(100)) #the output will be 2

print(math.factorial(5)) #the output will be 120

Exercise

Write a python program that uses math functions from the math module to perform the following: a. Square of 34

b. Log1010000

c. Cos 45 x sin 90

d. Exponent of 20

Lists in Python

We create a list in Python by placing items called elements inside square brackets separated by commas. The items in a list can be of a mixed data type.

Start IDLE.

Navigate to the File menu and click New Window.

Type the following:

list_mine=[] #empty list list_mine=[2,5,8] #list of integers list_mine=[5,"Happy", 5.2] #list having mixed data types

Assignment

Write a program that captures the following in a list: "Best", 26,89,3.9

Nested Lists

A nested list is a list as an item in another list.

Example

Start IDLE.

Navigate to the File menu and click New Window.

Type the following:

list_mine=["carrot", [9, 3, 6], ['g']]

Exercise

Write a nested for the following elements: [36,2,1],"Writer",'t',[3.0, 2.5]

Accessing Elements from a List

In programming and Python specifically, the first time is always indexed zero. For a list of five items, we will access them from index0 to index4. Failure to access the items in a list in this manner will create an index error. The index is always an integer as using other number types will create a type error. For nested lists, they are accessed via nested indexing.

Example

Start IDLE.

Navigate to the File menu and click New Window.

Type the following:

list_mine=['b','e','s','t']

print(list_mine[0]) #the output will be b print(list_mine[2]) #the output will be s print(list_mine[3]) #the output will be t *Exercise*

Given the following list:

your_collection=['t','k','v','w','z','n','f']

a. Create a program in Python to display the second item in the list b. Create a program in Python to display the sixth item in the last c. Create a program in Python to display the last item in the list.

Nested List Indexing
Start IDLE.

Navigate to the File menu and click New Window.

Type the following:

nested_list=["Best',[4,7,2,9]]

print(nested_list[0][1])

Python Negative Indexing
For its sequences, Python allows negative indexing. The last item on the list is index-1, index -2 is the second last item, and so on.

Start IDLE.

Navigate to the File menu and click New Window.

Type the following:

list_mine=['c','h','a','n','g','e','s']

print(list_mine[-1]) #Output is s print(list_mine [-4]) ##Output is n Slicing Lists in Python

Slicing operator (full colon) is used to access a range of elements in a list.
Example

Start IDLE.

Navigate to the File menu and click New Window.

Type the following:

list_mine=['c','h','a','n','g','e','s']

print(list_mine[3:5]) #Picking elements from the 4 to the sixth

Example

Picking elements from start to the fifth Start IDLE.

Navigate to the File menu and click New Window.

Type the following:

print(list_mine[:-6])

Example

Picking the third element to the last.

print(list_mine[2:])

Exercise

Given class_names=['John', 'Kelly', 'Yvonne', 'Una','Lovy','Pius', 'Tracy']

a. Write a python program using a slice operator to display from the second students and the rest.

b. Write a python program using a slice operator to display the first student to the third using a negative indexing feature.

c. Write a python program using a slice operator to display the fourth and fifth students only.

Manipulating Elements in a List using the assignment operator

Items in a list can be changed meaning lists are mutable.

Start IDLE.

Navigate to the File menu and click New Window.

Type the following:

list_yours=[4,8,5,2,1]

list_yours[1]=6

print(list_yours) #The output will be [4,6,5,2,1]

Changing a range of items in a list

Start IDLE.

Navigate to the File menu and click New Window.

Type the following:

list_yours[0:3]=[12,11,10] #Will change first item to fourth item in the list print(list_yours) #Output will be: [12,11,10,1]

Appending/Extending items in the List

The append() method allows extending the items in the list. The extend() can also be used.

Example

Start IDLE.

Navigate to the File menu and click New Window.

Type the following:

list_yours=[4, 6, 5]

list_yours.append(3)

print(list_yours) #The output will be [4,6,5, 3]

Example

Start IDLE.

Navigate to the File menu and click New Window.

Type the following:

list_yours=[4,6,5]

list_yours.extend([13,7,9]) print(list_yours) #The output will be [4,6,5,13,7,9]

The plus operator(+) can also be used to combine two lists. The * operator can be used to perform an iteration of a list of given several.

Example

Start IDLE.

Navigate to the File menu and click New Window.

Type the following:

list_yours=[4,6,5]

print(list yours+[13,7,9]) # Output:[4, 6, 5,13,7,9]

print(['happy']*4) #Output:["happy","happy", "happy","happy"]

Removing or Deleting Items from a List

The keyword del is used to delete elements or the entire list in Python.

Example

Start IDLE.

Navigate to the File menu and click New Window.

Type the following:

list_mine=['t','r','o','g','r','a','m']

del list_mine[1]

print(list_mine) #t, o, g, r, a, m

Deleting Multiple Elements

Example

Start IDLE.

Navigate to the File menu and click New Window.

Type the following:

del list_mine[0:3]

Example

print(list_mine) #a, m

Delete Entire List

Start IDLE.

Navigate to the File menu and click New Window.

Type the following:

delete list_mine

print(list_mine) #will generate an error of lost not found The remove() method or pop() function may be used to remove the specified item. The pop() method will remove and return the last item if the index is not given and helps implement lists as stacks. The clear() method is used to empty a list.

Start IDLE.

Navigate to the File menu and click New Window.

Type the following:

list_mine=['t','k','b','d','w','q','v']

list_mine.remove('t')

print(list_mine) #output will be ['t','k','b','d','w','q','v']

print(list_mine.pop(1)) #output will be 'k'

print(list_mine.pop()) #output will be 'v'

Assignment

Given list_yours=['K','N','O','C','K','E','D']

a. Pop the third item in the list, save the program as list1.

b. Remove the fourth item using remove() method and save the program as list2

c. Delete the second item in the list and save the program as list3.

d. Pop the list without specifying an index and save the program as list4.

Using Empty List to Delete an entire or specific element

Start IDLE.

Navigate to the File menu and click New Window.

Type the following:

list_mine=['t','k','b','d','w','q','v']

list_mine=[1:2]=[]

print(list_mine) #Output will be ['t','w','q','v']

List Methods in Python
Assignment

Use list access methods to display the following items in reversed order list_yours=[4,9,2,1,6,7]

Use list access method to count the elements in a.

Use the list access method to sort the items in a. in an ascending order/default.

Inbuilt Python Functions that can be used to manipulate Python Lists

In Python, lists are collections of data types that can be changed, organized, and include duplicate values. Lists are written within square brackets, as shown in the syntax below.

X = ["string001", "string002", "string003"]

print (X)

The same concept of position applies to Lists as the string data type, which dictates that the first string is considered to be at position 0. Subsequently, the strings that will follow are given positions 1, 2, and so on. You can selectively display the desired string from a List by referencing the position of that string inside the square bracket in the print command, as shown below.

X = ["string001", "string002", "string003"]

print (X [2])

OUTPUT – [string003]

Similarly, the concept of *negative indexing* is also applied to Python List. Let's look at the example below:

X = ["string001", "string002", "string003"]

print (X [-2])

OUTPUT – [string002]

You will also be able to specify a *range of indexes* by indicating the start and end of a range. The result in values of such command on a Python List would be a new List containing only the indicated items. Here is an example for your reference.

X = ["string001", "string002", "string003", "string004", "string005", "string006"]

print (X [2 : 4])

OUTPUT – ["string003", "string004"]

* Remember the first item is at position 0, and the final position of the range (4) is not included.

Now, if you do not indicate the start of this range, it will default to the position 0 as shown in the example below:

X = ["string001", "string002", "string003", "string004", "string005", "string006"]

print (X [: 3])

OUTPUT – ["string001", "string002", "string003"]

Similarly, if you do not indicate the end of this range it will display all the items of the List from the indicated start range to the end of the List, as shown in the example below:

X = ["string001", "string002", "string003", "string004", "string005", "string006"] print (X [3 :])

OUTPUT – ["string004", "string005", "string006"]

You can also specify a *range of negative indexes* to Python Lists, as shown in the example below: X = ["string001", "string002", "string003", "string004", "string005", "string006"]

print (X [-3 : -1])

OUTPUT – ["string004", "string005"]

* Remember the last item is at position -1, and the final position of this range (-1) is not included in the Output.

There might be instances when you need to *change the data value* for a Python List. This can be accomplished by referring to the index number of that item and declaring the new value. Let's look at the example below: X = ["string001", "string002", "string003", "string004", "string005", "string006"]

X [3] = "newstring"

print (X)

OUTPUT – ["string001", "string002", "string003", "newstring", "string005", "string006"]

You can also determine the *length* of a Python List using the "len()" function, as shown in the example below: X = ["string001", "string002", "string003", "string004", "string005", "string006"] print (len (X))

OUTPUT – 6

Python Lists can also be changed by *adding new items* to an existing list using the built-in "append ()" method, as shown in the example below: X = ["string001", "string002", "string003", "string004"]

X.append ("newstring")

print (X)

OUTPUT – ["string001", "string002", "string003", "string004", "newstring"]

You can also, add a new item to an existing Python List at a specific position using the built-in "insert ()" method, as shown in the example below: X = ["string001", "string002", "string003", "string004"]

X.insert (2, "newstring")

print (X)

OUTPUT – ["string001", "string002", "newstring", "string004"]

there might be instances when you need to *copy* an existing Python List. This can be accomplished by using the built-in "copy ( )" method or the "list ( )" method, as shown in the example below: *X = ["string001", "string002", "string003", "string004", "string005", "string006"]*

Y = X.copy( )

print (Y)

OUTPUT − ["string001", "string002", "string003", "string004", "string005", "string006"]

X = ["string001", "string002", "string003", "string004", "string005", "string006"]

Y = list (X)

print (Y)

OUTPUT − ["string001", "string002", "string003", "string004", "string005", "string006"]

There are multiple built-in methods to *delete items* from a Python List.

- To selectively delete a specific item, the "remove ()" method can be used.

X = ["string001", "string002", "string003", "string004"]

X.remove ("string002")

print (X)

OUTPUT - ["string001", "string003", "string004"]

- To delete a specific item from the List, the "pop ()" method can be used with the position of the value. If no index has been indicated, the last item of the index will be removed.

X = ["string001", "string002", "string003", "string004"]

X.pop ( )

print (X)

OUTPUT - ["string001", "string002", "string003"]

- To delete a specific index from the List, the "del ()" method can be used, followed by the index within square brackets.

X = ["string001", "string002", "string003", "string004"]

del X [2]

print (X)

OUTPUT - ["string001", "string002", "string004"]

- To delete the entire List variable, the "del ()" method can be used, as shown below.

X = ["string001", "string002", "string003", "string004"]

del X

OUTPUT - …..

- To delete all the string values from the List without deleting the variable itself, the "clear ()" method can be used, as shown below.

X = ["string001", "string002", "string003", "string004"]

X.clear()

print (X)

OUTPUT – [ ]

Concatenation of Lists

You can join multiple lists with the use of the "+" logical operator or by adding all the items from one list to another using the "append ( )" method. The "extend ( )" method can be used to add a list at the end of another list. Let's look at the examples below to understand these commands.

X = ["string001", "string002", "string003", "string004"]

Y = [10, 20, 30, 40]

Z = X + Y

print (Z)

OUTPUT – ["string001", "string002", "string003", "string004", 10, 20, 30, 40]

X = ["string001", "string002", "string003", "string004"]

Y = [10, 20, 30, 40]

For x in Y:

X.append (x)

print (X)

OUTPUT – ["string001", "string002", "string003", "string004", 10, 20, 30, 40]

X = ["string001", "string002", "string003"]

Y = [10, 20, 30]

X.extend (Y)

print (X)

OUTPUT – ["string001", "string002", "string003", 10, 20, 30]

Exercise

Create a list "A" with string data values as "red, olive, cyan, lilac, mustard" and display the item at -2 position.

Use Your Discretion Here And Write Your Code First

Now, check your code against the correct code below:

$A = I$"red", "olive", "cyan", "lilac", "mustard"]

print (A [-2])

OUTPUT – ["lilac"]

Exercise

Create a list "A" with string data values as "red, olive, cyan, lilac, mustard" and display the items ranging from the string on the second position to the end of the string.

Use Your Discretion Here And Write Your Code First

Now, check your code against the correct code below:

A = ["red", "olive", "cyan", "lilac", "mustard"]

print (A [2 :])

OUTPUT – ["cyan", "lilac", "mustard"]

Exercise

Create a list "A" with string data values as "red, olive, cyan, lilac, mustard" and replace the string "olive" to "teal".

Use Your Discretion Here And Write Your Code First

Now, check your code against the correct code below:

A = ["red", "olive", "cyan", "lilac", "mustard"]

A [1] = ["teal"]

print (A)

OUTPUT – ["red", "teal", "cyan", "lilac", "mustard"]

Exercise

Create a list "A" with string data values as "red, olive, cyan, lilac, mustard" and copy the list "A" to create a list "B".

Use Your Discretion Here And Write Your Code First

Now, check your code against the correct code below:

A = ["red", "olive", "cyan", "lilac", "mustard"]

B = A.copy ( )

print (B)

OUTPUT – ["red", "olive", "cyan", "lilac", "mustard"]

Exercise

Create a list "A" with string data values as "red, olive, cyan, lilac, mustard" and delete the strings "red" and "lilac".

Use Your Discretion Here And Write Your Code First

Now, check your code against the correct code below:

A = ["red", "olive", "cyan", "lilac", "mustard"]

del.A [0, 2]

print (A)

OUTPUT – ["olive", "cyan", "mustard"]

String in Python

Python strings are competent to usually make use of single or double quotation marks, plus you're in a position to utilize quotation marks of only one type in a string using an additional kind, consequently, the following is valid:

This is a valid' string

Multi-strings are enclosed in specific or perhaps triple two-fold quotes. Python can support Unicode immediately, using the following syntax:

Flow management statements Python's flow management statements are while', for' and if'. For a switch, you've to use if'. For enumerating by show participants, use for'. For getting a choice checklist, use range (amount). Here is the declaration syntax: range list = range(10)

>>>; print range list

[0, 8, 7, 6, 5, 4, 3, 2, 1, 9]

for quantity in range list:

if the number in (three, 7, 4, 9):

break

else:

continue

else:

pass

if perhaps rangelist[1] == 2:

print The next item (lists are 0 based) is 2

Elif rangelist[1] == 3:

print The next item (lists are 0 based) is 3

else:

print documents Dunno

while rangelist[1] == 1:

pass

Example

Start IDLE.

Navigate to the File menu and click New Window.

Type the following:

string_mine = 'Colorful'

print(string_mine)

string_mine = "Hello"

print(string_mine)

string_mine = '''Hello'''

print(string_mine)

string_mine = """"I feel like I have been born a programmer""""

print(string_mine)

Accessing items in a string

Example

Start IDLE.

Navigate to the File menu and click New Window.

Type the following:

str = 'Colorful'

print('str = ', str)

print('str[1] = ', str[1]) #Output the second item print('str[-2] = ', str[-2]) #Output the second last item print('str[2:4] = ', str[2:4]) #Output the third through the fifth item

Deleting or Changing in Python

In Python, strings are immutable therefore cannot be changed once assigned. However, deleting the entire string is possible.

Example

Start IDLE.

Navigate to the File menu and click New Window.

Type the following:

del string_mine

String Operations

Several operations can be performed on a string making it a widely used data type in Python.

Concatenation using the + operator, repetition using the * operator
Example

Start IDLE.

Navigate to the File menu and click New Window.

Type the following:

string1='Welcome'

string2='Again'

print('string1+string2=',string1+string2) print(' string1 * 3 =', string1 * 3) Exercise

Given string_a=" I am awake" and string_b="coding in Python in a pajama"

String Iteration

The for-control statement is used to continually scan through an entire scan until the specified several are reached before terminating the scan.

Example

Start IDLE.

Navigate to the File menu and click New Window.

Type the following:

Membership Test in String

The keyword is used to test if a substring exists.

Example

't' in "triumph' #Will return True Inbuilt Python Functions for working with Strings They include enumerate () and len().The len() function returns the length of the string.

String Formatting in Python

Escape Sequences Single and Double Quotes

Example

Start IDLE.

Navigate to the File menu and click New Window.

Type the following:

print('They said, "We need a new team?"') # escape with single quotes # escaping double quotes

print("They said, \" We need a new team\")

Escape Sequences in Python

The escape sequences enable us to format our output to enhance clarity to the human user.

A program will still run successfully without using escape sequences but the output will be highly confusing to the human user.

Writing and displaying output in expected output is part of good programming practices.

The following are commonly used escape sequences.

Examples

Start IDLE.

Navigate to the File menu and click New Window.

Type the following:

print("D:\\Lessons\\Programming") print("Prints\n in two lines")

Working with Files

Programs are made with input and output in mind.

You input data to the program, the program processes the input, and it ultimately provides you with output.

For example, a calculator will take in numbers and operations you want.

It will then process the operation you wanted.

And then, it will display the result to you as its output.

There are multiple ways for a program to receive input and to produce output.

One of those ways is to read and write data on files.

To start learning how to work with files, you need to learn the open() function.

The open() function has one *required* parameter and two *optional* parameters.

The first and required parameter is the file name.

The second parameter is the access mode. And the third parameter is buffering or buffer size.

The filename parameter requires string data.

The access mode requires string data, but there is a set of string values that you can use and is defaulted to "r".

The buffer size parameter requires an integer and is defaulted to 0.

To practice using the open() function, create a file with the name sampleFile.txt inside your Python directory.

Try this sample code:

```
>>> file1 = open("sampleFile.txt")
>>> _
```

Note that the file function returns a file object.

The statement in the example assigns the file object to variable file1.

The file object has multiple attributes, and three of them are:

name: This contains the name of the file.

mode: This contains the access mode you used to access the file.

closed: This returns False if the file has been opened and True if the file is closed. When you use the open() function, the file is set to open.

Now, access those attributes.

```
>>> file1 = open("sampleFile.txt")
>>> file1.name
'sampleFile.txt'
>>> file1.mode
'r'
>>> file1.closed
False
>>> _
```

Whenever you are finished with a file, close them using the close() method.

```
>>> file1 = open("sampleFile.txt")
>>> file1.closed
False
>>> file1.close()
>>> file1.closed
True
>>> _
```

Remember that closing the file does not delete the variable or object.

To reopen the file, just open and reassign the file object.

For example:

```
>>> file1 = open("sampleFile.txt")

>>> file1.close()

>>> file1 = open(file1.name)

>>> file1.closed
False

>>> _
```

Reading from a File

Before proceeding, open the sampleFile.txt in your text editor.

Type "Hello World" in it and save.

Go back to Python.

To read the contents of the file, use the read() method.

For example:

```
>>> file1 = open("sampleFile.txt")

>>> file1.read()
'Hello World'

>>> _
```

File Pointer

Whenever you access a file, Python sets the file pointer.

The file pointer is like your word processor's cursor.

Any operation on the file starts at where the file pointer is.

When you open a file, and when it is set to the default access mode, which is "r" (read-only), the file pointer is set at the beginning of the file.

To know the current position of the file pointer, you can use the tell() method.

For example:

\>>> file1 = open("sampleFile.txt")

\>>> file1.tell()

0

\>>> _

Most of the actions you perform on the file move the file pointer.

For example:

\>>> file1 = open("sampleFile.txt")

\>>> file1.tell()

0

```
>>> file1.read()
```

'Hello World'

```
>>> file1.tell()
```

11

```
>>> file1.read()
```

''

```
>>>
```

To move the file pointer to a position you desire, you can use the seek() function.

For example:

```
>>> file1 = open("sampleFile.txt")
>>> file1.tell()
```

0

```
>>> file1.read()
```

'Hello World'

```
>>> file1.tell()
```

11

```
>>> file1.seek(0)
```

0

>>> file1.read()

'Hello World'

>>> file1.seek(1)

1

>>> file1.read()

'ello World'

>>> _

The seek() method has two parameters.

The first is offset, which sets the pointer's position depending on the second parameter.

Also, an argument for this parameter is required.

The second parameter is optional.

It is for whence, which dictates where the "seek" will start.

It is set to 0 by default.

If set to 0, Python will set the pointer's position to the offset argument.

If set to 1, Python will set the pointer's position relative or in addition to the current position of the pointer.

If set to 2, Python will set the pointer's position relative or in addition to the file's end.

Note that the last two options require the access mode to have binary access. If the access mode does not have binary access, the last two options will be useful to determine the current position of the pointer [seek(0, 1)] and the position at the end of the file [seek(0, 2)].

For example:

>>> file1 = open("sampleFile.txt")

>>> file1.tell()

0

>>> file1.seek(1)

1

>>> file1.seek(0, 1)

0

>>> file1.seek(0, 2)

11

>>> _

File Access Modes

To write to a file, you will need to know more about file access modes in Python.

There are three types of file operations: reading, writing and appending.

Reading allows you to access and copy any part of the file's content.

Writing allows you to overwrite a file's contents and create a new one.

Appending allows you to write on the file while keeping the other content intact.

There are two types of file access modes: string and binary.

String access allows you to access a file's content as if you are opening a text file.

Binary access allows you to access a file on its rawest form: binary.

In your sample file, accessing it using string access allows you to read the line "Hello World".

Accessing the file using binary access will let you read "Hello World" in binary, which will be b'Hello World'.

For example:

>>> x = open("sampleFile.txt", "rb")

```
>>> x.read()

b'Hello World'

>>> _
```

String access is useful for editing text files.

Binary access is useful for anything else, like pictures, compressed files, and executables. In this book, you will only be taught how to handle text files.

There are multiple values that you can enter in the file access mode parameter of the open() function.

But you do not need to memorize the combination.

You just need to know the letter combinations.

Each letter and symbol stand for an access mode and operation.

For example:

r = read-only—file pointer placed at the beginning

r+ = read and write

a = append—file pointer placed at the end

a+ = read and append

w = overwrite/create—file pointer set to 0 since you create the file

w+ = read and overwrite/create

b = binary

By default, file access mode is set to string.

You need to add b to allow binary access.

For example "rb".

Writing to a File

When writing to a file, you must always remember that Python overwrites and does not insert files.

For example:

>>> x = open("sampleFile.txt", "r+")

>>> x.read()

'Hello World'

>>> x.tell(0)

0

>>> x.write("text")

4

>>> x.tell()

4

```
>>> x.read()

'o World'

>>> x.seek(0)

0

>>> x.read()

'texto World'

>>> _
```

You might have expected that the resulting text will be "textHello World".

The write method of the file object replaces each character one by one, starting from the current position of the pointer.

Practice Exercise

For practice, you need to perform the following tasks:

Create a new file named test.txt.

Write the entire practice exercise instructions on the file.

Close the file and reopen it.

Read the file and set the cursor back to 0.

Close the file and open it using append access mode.

Add a rewritten version of these instructions at the end of the file.

Create a new file and put similar content to it by copying the contents of the test.txt file.

Working with files in Python is easy to understand but difficult to implement.

As you already saw, there are only a few things that you need to remember.

The hard part is when you are accessing the file.

Remember that the key things that you should master are the access modes and the management of the file pointer.

It is easy to get lost in a file that contains a thousand characters.

Aside from being versed in the file operations, you should also supplement your learning with the functions and methods of the str class in Python.

Most of the time, you will be dealing with strings if you need to work on a file.

Do not worry about binary yet.

That is a different beast altogether and you will only need to tame it when you are already adept at Python. As a beginner, expect that you will not deal yet with binary files that often contain media information.

Anyway, the next lesson is an elaboration on the "try" and "except" statements.

You'll discover how to manage and handle errors and exceptions effectively.

Python Tuples

In Python, Tuples are collections of data types that cannot be changed but can be arranged in a specific order. Tuples allow for duplicate items and are written within round brackets, as shown in the syntax below.

Tuple = ("string001", "string002", "string003")

print (Tuple)

Tuples are similar to lists and creating them is quite simple, one has to put commas to separate values and these values can also be enclosed in parenthesis. For example: *tup1 = ('chemistry', 'physics', 1998, 2000); tup2 = (7, 8, 9); tup3 = "x", "y", "z" ; Listed below are some of the basic features of tuple:*

a) For writing an empty tuple two parentheses are used – ***tup1 = ();***

b) Even of the tuple contains a single value one has to include comma—***tup1 = (50,);***

c) The indices in tuple start with at 0 and slicing can also be done.

d) Square brackets are used to access values in tuples

e) One cannot change or update the values in tuples

f) Removing the tuple element is not possible; however one can use *del* to remove the entire tuple.

g) All general operators can be used There are few built-in tuples like:

For comparing different elements - cmp(tuple1, tuple2)

To find the total length of tuple -len(tuple)

Converting a list to tuple – tuple(seq)

Find maximum value—max(tuple)

Minimum value – min(tuple)

Similar to the Python List, you can selectively display the desired string from a Tuple by referencing the position of that string inside the square bracket in the print command as shown below.

Tuple = ("string001", "string002", "string003")

print (Tuple [1])

OUTPUT – ("string002")

The concept of *negative indexing* can also be applied to Python Tuple, as shown in the example below: *Tuple = ("string001", "string002", "string003", "string004", "string005")*

print (Tuple [-2])

OUTPUT – ("string004")

You will also be able to specify a *range of indexes* by indicating the start and end of a range. The result in values of such command on a Python Tuple would be a new Tuple containing only the indicated items, as shown in the example below:

Tuple = ("string001", "string002", "string003", "string004", "string005", "string006")

print (Tuple [1:5])

Output

("string002", "string003", "string004", "string005")

* Remember the first item is at position 0 and the final position of the range, which is the fifth position in this example, is not included.

You can also specify a **range of negative indexes** *to Python Tuples, as shown in the example below:* Tuple = ("string001", "string002", "string003", "string004", "string005", "string006")

print (Tuple [-4: -2])

Output – ("string004", "string005")

* Remember the last item is at position -1 and the final position of this range, which is the negative fourth position in this example is not included in the Output.

Unlike Python lists, you cannot directly *change the data value of Python Tuples* after they have been created. However, conversion of a Tuple into a List and then modifying the data value of that List will allow you to subsequently create a Tuple from that updated List. Let's look at the example below: Tuple1 = *("string001", "string002", "string003", "string004", "string005", "string006") List1 = list (Tuple1)*

List1 [2] = "update this list to create new tuple"

Tuple1 = tuple (List1)

print (Tuple1)

Output – ("string001", "string002", "update this list to create new tuple", "string004", "string005", "string006")

You can also determine the *length* of a Python Tuple using the "len()" function, as shown in the example below: **Tuple = ("string001", "string002", "string003", "string004", "string005", "string006")**

print (len (Tuple))

Output – **6**

You cannot selectively delete items from a Tuple, but you can use the "del" keyword to *delete the Tuple* in its entirety, as shown in the example below: Tuple = *("string001", "string002", "string003", "string004")* del Tuple

print (Tuple)

Output – name 'Tuple' is not defined

You can *join multiple Tuples* with the use of the "+" logical operator.

Tuple1 = ("string001", "string002", "string003", "string004")

Tuple2 = (100, 200, 300)

Tuple3 = Tuple1 + Tuple2

print (Tuple3)

Output – ("string001", "string002", "string003", "string004", 100, 200, 300)

You can also use the "tuple ( )" constructor to create a Tuple, as shown in the example below:

Tuple1 = tuple (("string001", "string002", "string003", "string004"))

print (Tuple1)

Example
Start IDLE.

Navigate to the File menu and click New Window.

Type the following:

tuple_mine = (21, 12, 31)

print(tuple_mine)

tuple_mine = (31, "Green", 4.7) print(tuple_mine)

Accessing Python Tuple Elements *Example*

Start IDLE.

Navigate to the File menu and click New Window.

Type the following:

tuple_mine=['t','r','o','g','r','a','m']

print(tuple_mine[1]) #output:'r'

print(tuple_mine[3]) #output:'g'

Negative Indexing

Just like lists, tuples can also be indexed negatively.

Like lists, -1 refers to the last element on the list and -2 refers to the second last element.

Example

Start IDLE.

Navigate to the File menu and click New Window.

Type the following:

tuple_mine=['t','r','o','g','r','a','m']

print(tuple_mine [-2]) #the output will be 'a'

Slicing

The slicing operator, the full colon is used to access a range of items in a tuple.

Example

Start IDLE.

Navigate to the File menu and click New Window.

Type the following:

tuple_mine=['t','r','o','g','r','a','m']

print(tuple_mine [2:5]) #Output: 'o','g','r','a'

print(tuple_mine[:-4]) #'g','r','a','m'

Note

Tuple elements are immutable meaning they cannot be changed. However, we can combine elements in a tuple using +(concatenation operator). We can also repeat elements in a tuple using the * operator, just like lists.

Example

Start IDLE.

Navigate to the File menu and click New Window.

Type the following:

print((7, 45, 13) + (17, 25, 76)) print(("Several",) * 4) *Note*

Since we cannot change elements in a tuple, we cannot delete the elements too.

However, removing the full tuple can be attained using the keyword del.

Example

Start IDLE.

Navigate to the File menu and click New Window.

Type the following:

t_mine=['t','k','q','v','y','c','d']

del t_mine

Available Tuple Methods in Python

There are only two methods available for working Python tuples.

count(y)

When called will give the item numbers that are equal to y.

index(y)

When called will give the index first item index that is equal to y.

Example

Start IDLE.

Navigate to the File menu and click New Window.

Type the following:

t_mine=['t','k','q','v','y','c','d']

print(t_mine.count('t'))

print(t_mine.index('l'))

Testing Membership in Tuple

The keyword in us used to check the specified element exists in a tuple.

Start IDLE.

Navigate to the File menu and click New Window.

Type the following:

t_mine=['t','k','q','v','y','c','d']

print('a' t_mine) #Output: True print('k' in t_mine) #Output: False

Exercise

Create a Tuple "X" with string data values as "pies, cake, bread, scone, cookies" and display the item at -3 position.

Use Your Discretion Here And Write Your Code First

Now, check your code against the correct code below:

X = ("pies", "cake", "bread", "scone", "cookies")

print (X [-3])

Output – ("bread")

Exercise

Create a Tuple "X" with string data values as "pies, cake, bread, scone, cookies" and display items ranging from -2 to -4.

Use Your Discretion Here And Write Your Code First

Now, check your code against the correct code below:

X = ("pies", "cake", "bread", "scone", "cookies")

print (X [-4 : -2])

Output – ("cake", "bread")

Exercise

Create a Tuple "X" with string data values as "pies, cake, bread, scone, cookies" and change its item from "cookies" to "start" using the List function.

Use Your Discretion Here And Write Your Code First

Now, check your code against the correct code below:

X = ("pies", "cake", "bread", "scone", "cookies")

Y = list (X)

Y [4] = "tart"

X = tuple (Y)

print (X)

Output – ("pies", "cake", "bread", "scone", "tart")

Exercise

Create a Tuple "X" with string data values as "pies, cake, cookies" and another Tuple "Y" with numeric data values as (2, 12, 22), then join them together.

Use Your Discretion Here And Write Your Code First

Now, check your code against the correct code below:

X = ("pies", "cake", "cookies")

Y = (2, 12, 22)

Z = X + Y

print (Z)

Output – ("pies", "cake", "cookies", 2, 12, 22)

Python Sets

In Python, Sets are collections of data types that cannot be organized and indexed. Sets do not allow for duplicate items and must be written within curly brackets, as shown in the syntax below: *set = {"string1", "string2", "string3"}*

print (set)

Unlike the Python List and Tuple, you cannot selectively display desired items from a Set by referencing the position of that item because the Python Set is not arranged in any order. Therefore, items do not have any indexing. However, the "for" loop can be used on Sets (more on this topic later in this chapter).

Unlike Python Lists, you cannot directly *change the data values of Python Sets* after they have been created. However, you can use the "add ()" method to add a single item to Set and use the "update ( )" method to add one or more items to an already existing Set. Let's look at the example below: *set = {"string1", "string2", "string3"}*

set. add ("newstring")

print (set)

Output – {"string1", "string2", "string3", "newstring"}

set = {"string1", "string2", "string3"}

set. update (["newstring1", "newstring2", "newstring3",)

print (set)

Output – {"string1", "string2", "string3", "newstring1", "newstring2", "newstring3"}

You can also determine the *length* of a Python Set using the "len()" function, as shown in the example below: *set = {"string1", "string2", "string3", "string4", "string5", "string6", "string7"}*

print (len(set))

Output – 7

To selectively delete a specific item from a Set, the "remove ()" method can be used as shown in the code below: *set = {"string1", "string2", "string3", "string4", "string5"}*

set. remove ("string4")

print (set)

Output – {"string1", "string2", "string3", *"string5"}*

You can also use the "discard ( )" method to delete specific items from a Set, as shown in the example below:

set = {"string1", "string2", "string3", "string4", "string5"}

set. discard ("string3")

print (set)

Output – {"string1", "string2", "string4", *"string5"}*

The "pop ( )" method can be used to selectively delete only the last item of a Set. It must be noted here that since the Python Sets are unordered, any item that the system deems as the last item will be removed. As a result, the output of this method will be the item that has been removed.

set = {"string1", "string2", "string3", "string4", "string5"}

A = set.pop ( )

print (A)

print (set)

Output –

String2

{"string1", "string3", "string4", *"string5"}*

To delete the entire Set, the "del" keyword can be used, as shown below.

set = {"string1", "string2", "string3", "string4", "string5"}

delete set

print (set)

Output – name 'set' is not defined

To delete all the items from the Set without deleting the variable itself, the "clear ()" method can be used, as shown below: *set = {"string1", "string2", "string3", "string4", "string5"}*

set.clear ( )

print (set)

Output – set ( )

You can join multiple Sets with the use of the "union ( )" method. The output of this method will be a new set that contains all items from both the sets. You can also use the "update ( )" method to insert all the items from one set into another without creating a new Set.

Set1 = {"string1", "string2", "string3", "string4", "string5"}

Set2 = {15, 25, 35, 45, 55}

Set3 = Set1.union (Set2)

print (Set3)

Output – {"string1", 15, "string2", 25, "string3", 35, "string4", 45, "string5", 55}

Set1 = {"string1", "string2", "string3", "string4", "string5"}

Set2 = {15, 25, 35, 45, 55}

Set1.update (Set2)

print (Set1)

Output – {25, "string1", 15, "string4",55, "string2", 35, "string3", 45, "string5"}

You can also use the "set ( )" constructor to create a Set, as shown in the example below:

Set1 = set (("string1", "string2", "string3", "string4", "string5"))

print (Set1)

Output – {"string3", "string5", "string2", "string4", "string1"}

Exercise

Create a Set "Veg" with string data values as "pies, cake, bread, scone, cookies" and add new items "tart", "custard" and "waffles" to this Set.

Use Your Discretion Here And Write Your Code First

Now, check your code against the correct code below:

Veg = {"pies", "cake", "bread", "scone", "cookies"}

Veg.update (["tart", "custard", "waffles"])

print (Veg)

Output – {"pies", "custard", "scone", "cake", "bread", "waffles", "cookies", "tart"}

Exercise

Create a Set "Veg" with string data values as "pies, cake, bread, scone, cookies", then delete the last item from this Set.

Use Your Discretion Here And Write Your Code First

Now, check your code against the correct code below:

Veg = {"pies", "cake", "bread", "scone", "cookies"}

X = Veg.pop ( )

print (X)

print (Veg)

Output –

bread

{"pies", "scone", "cake", "cookies"}

Exercise

Create a Set "Veg" with string data values as "pies, cake, bread, scone, cookies" and another Set "Veg2" with items as "tart, eggs, custard, waffles". Then combine both these Sets to create a third new Set.

Use Your Discretion Here And Write Your Code First

Now, check your code against the correct code below:

Veg = {"pies", "cake", "bread", "scone", "cookies"}

Veg2 = {"tart", "eggos", "custard", "waffles"}

AllVeg = Veg.union (Veg2) #this Set name may vary as it has not been defined in the exercise

print (AllVeg)

Output – {"pies", "custard", "scone", "cake", "eggos", "bread", "waffles", "cookies", "tart"}

Functions

We began with almost no prior knowledge about Python except for a clue that it was some kind of programming language that is in great demand these days. Now, look at you; creating simple programs, executing codes, and fixing small-scale problems on your own. Not bad at all!

However, learning always comes to a point where things can get rather trickier.

In quite a similar fashion, Functions are docile looking things; you call them when you need to get something done. But did you know that these functions have so much going on at the back? Imagine every function as a mini-program. It is also written by programmers like us to carry out specific things without having to write lines and lines of codes. You only do it once, save it as a function, and then just call the function where it is applicable or needed.

The time has come for us to dive into a complex world of functions where we don't just learn how to use them effectively, but we also look into what goes on behind these functions, and how we can come up with our very own personalized function. This will be slightly challenging, but I promise, there are more references that you will enjoy keeping the momentum going.

Understanding Functions Better

Functions are like containers that store lines and lines of codes within themselves, just like a variable that contains one specific value. There are two types of functions we get to deal with within Python. The first ones are built-in or predefined, the others are custom-made or user-created functions.

Either way, each function has a specific task that it can carry out. The code that is written before creating any function is what gives that function identity and a task. Now, the function knows what it needs to do whenever it is called in. When we began our journey, we wrote "I made it!" on the console as our first program? We used our first function there as well: the print() function. Functions are generally identified by parentheses that follow the name of the function. Within these parentheses, we pass arguments called parameters. Some functions accept a certain kind of parenthesis while others accept different ones. Let us look a little deeper and see how functions greatly help us reduce our work and better organize our codes. Imagine, we have a program that runs during live streaming of an event. The purpose of the program is to provide our users with a customized greeting. Imagine just how many times you would need to write the same code again and again if there were quite a few users who decide to join your stream. With functions, you can cut down on your work easily.

To create a function, we first need to 'define' the same. That is where a keyword called 'def' comes along. When you start typing 'def' Python immediately knows you are about to define a function. You will see the color of the three letters change to orange (if using PyCharm as your IDE). That is another sign of confirmation that Python knows what you are about to do.

def say_hi():

Here, say_hi is the name I have decided to go with, you can choose any that you prefer. Remember, keep your name descriptive so that it is understandable and easy to read for anyone. After you have named your function, follow it up with parentheses. Lastly, add the friendly old colon to let Python know we are about to add a block of code. Press enter to start a new indented line.

Now, we shall print out two statements for every user who will join the stream.

print("Hello there!")

print('Welcome to My Live Stream!')

After this, give two lines of space to take away those wiggly lines that appear the minute you start typing something else. Now, to have this printed out easily, just call the function by typing its name and run the program. In our case, it would be: *say_hi()*

Output:

Hello there!

Welcome to My Live Stream!

See how easily this can work for us in the future? We do not have to repeat this over and over again. Let's make this function a little more interesting by giving it a parameter. Right at the top line, where it says "def say_hi()"? Let us add a parameter here. Type in the word 'name' as a parameter within the parenthesis. Now, the word should be greyed out to confirm that Python has understood the same as a parameter.

Now, you can use this to your advantage and further personalize the greetings to something like this:

```
def say_hi(name):

print(f"Hello there, {user}!")

print('Welcome to My Live Stream!')

user = input("Please enter your name to begin: ")

say_hi(user)
```

The output would now ask the user regarding their name. This will then be stored into a variable called user. Since this is a string value, say_hi() should be able to accept this easily. If you pass 'user' as an argument, we get this as an output: *Please enter your name to begin: Johnny*

Hello there, Johnny!

Welcome to My Live Stream!

Now that's more like it! Personalized to perfection. We can add as many lines as we want, the function will continue to update itself and provide greetings to various users with different names. There may be times where you may need more than just the user's first name. You might want to inquire about the last name of the user as well. To add to that, add this to the first line and follow the same accordingly: *def say_hi(first_name, last_name):*

```
print(f"Hello there, {first_name} {last_name}!")

print('Welcome to My Live Stream!')
```

first_name = input("Enter your first name: ")

last_name = input("Enter your last name: ")

say_hi(first_name, last_name)

Now, the program will begin by asking the user for their first name, followed by the last name. Once that is sorted, the program will provide a personalized greeting with both the first and last names.

However, these are positional arguments, meaning that each value you input is in order. If you were to change the positions of the names for John Doe, Doe will become the first name and John will become the last name. You may wish to remain a little careful about that.

Hopefully, now you have a good idea of what functions are and how you can access and create them. Now, we will jump towards a more complex front of 'return' statements.

"Wait! There's more?"

Well, I could have explained this earlier, but back then, when we were discussing statements, you may not have understood it completely. Since we have covered all the bases, it is appropriate enough for us to see exactly what these are and how these gel along with functions.

Return Statement

Return statements are useful when you wish to create functions whose sole job is to return some values. These could be for users or programmers alike.

It is a lot easier if we do this instead of talking about theories, so let's jump back to our PyCharm and create another function. Let us start by defining a function called 'cube' which will multiply the number by itself three times. However, since we want Python to return a value, we will use the following code: *def cube(number):*

return number number number

By typing 'return' you are informing Python that you wish for it to return a value to you that can later be stored in a variable or used elsewhere. It is pretty much like the input() function where a user enters something and it gets returned to us.

def cube(number):

return number number number

number = int(input("Enter the number: "))

print(cube(number))

Go ahead and try out the code to see how it works. We don't need to define such functions. You can create your complex functions that convert kilos into pounds, miles into kilometers, or even carry out far greater and more complex jobs. The only limit is your imagination. The more you practice, the more you explore. With that said, it is time to say goodbye to the world of functions and head into the advanced territories of Python. By now, you already have all you need to know to start writing your codes.

Random function in Python

Start IDLE.

Navigate to the File menu and click New Window.

Type the following:

import math

print(random.shuffle_num(11, 21)) y=['f','g','h','m']

print(random.pick(y))

random.anypic(y)

print(y)

print(your_pick.random())

CHAPTER 5:

OPERATION IN PYTHON

The Python Operators

The Python operators are going to be pretty diverse and can do a lot of different things in your code based on how you use them.

When we are talking about the operators, there are going to be quite a few different types that you can work within the code. Let's explore a bit more about these operators and how we can use these for our needs as well.

Arithmetic Operators

The first type of operator that we are going to take a look at is the arithmetic operators. These are going to be similar to the signals and signs that we would use when we do mathematical equations. You can work with the addition, subtraction, multiplication, and division symbols to do the same kinds of actions on the different parts of the code that you are working with. These are common when you want to do something like add two parts of the code together with one another. You have the freedom to add in as many of these to your code as you would like, and you can even put more than one type in the same statement. Just remember that you need to work with the rules of operation and do these in the right order to make it work the way that you would like. Otherwise, you will be able to add in as many of these to the same code as you need to make it work.

Let's suppose we have two variables whose values are $x = 16$, $y = 4$.

Operator	Description of the operator	Example
Addition (+)	This operator will be adding the values on both sides of operands.	$x + y = 20$
Subtraction (-)	This operator will be subtracting the right-hand side value from the left-hand side value of the operand.	$x - y = 12$

Multiplication (*)	This operator will be multiplying the two values on both sides of the operands.	x * y = 64
Division (/)	This operator will be dividing the left-hand side value by the right-hand side value of the operand.	x / y = 4
Modulus (%)	This operator will be dividing the left-hand side value by the right-hand side value of the operand and returns the remainder.	x % y = 0
Exponent (**)	This operator will be doing the 'exponential power' calculation on operands.	x ** y = 16 to the power 4
Floor division (//)	This operator will be dividing the operands, the quotient of a number which is divided by 2 is the result.	13 // 3 = 4, simultaneously 13.0 // 3.0 = 4.0;

The above is going to be some of the different operators that you can work with that fit into this category. Working with these will ensure that we can handle the work and that we will be able to use it inside of our codes.

Comparison Operators

After looking at the arithmetic operators, it is also possible for us to work with the comparison operators. These comparison operators are going to be good to work with because they will let you take over two, and sometimes more, values and statements in the code and then see how they are going to compare to one another. This is one that we will use often for a lot of codes that are going to rely on Boolean expressions because it ensures that the answer you get back will be false and true. So, your statements in this situation are going to be the same as each other, or they will be different. Let's take two variables having the values a = 20, b = 15:

Operator	Description of the operator	Example
(==)	This condition becomes true only if two given values (operands) are equal.	(a == b) ⍰ not true
(!=)	This condition becomes true only if the two operands aren't equal.	(a != b) ⍰ true
(>)	This condition becomes true only if the left operand is greater than the right operand.	(a > b) ⍰ true
(<)	This condition becomes true only if the right operand is greater than the left operand.	(a < b) ⍰ not true
(>=)	This condition becomes true only if the left operand is greater than or equal to the right operator.	(a >= b) ⍰ true
(<=)	This condition becomes true only if the right operand is greater than or equal to the left operand.	(a <= b) ⍰ not true

There are a lot of times when we are going to be able to work with these comparison operators to get the most out of the programming that we are doing. You need to consider these ahead of time and make sure that we are going to be able to get the results that we need in our code.

Logical Operators

Next, we are going to be looking at the logical operators. These may not be used as often as the other options, but it is still some time for us to look it over. These operators are going to be used when it is time to evaluate the input that a user can present to us, with any of the conditions that you can set in your code. There are going to be three types of logical operators that we can work with, and some of the examples that you are going to use to work with this in your code include:

And: if x ends up being the false one, the compiler is going to evaluate it. If x ends up being true, it will move on and evaluate y.

Not: if it ends up being false, the compiler is going to return True. But if x ends up being true, the program will return false.

A	B	A AND B	A OR B	NOT
False	False	False	False	True
False	True	False	True	True
True	False	False	True	False
True	True	True	True	False

The chart above is going to show us a bit more about the logical operators that we can work with as well. This can give us a good idea of what is going to happen when we use each of the operators for our own needs as well.

Assignment Operators

And the final type of operator that we are going to take a look at is the assignment operator. This is going to be the kind of operator that will show up, and if you take a look at some of the different codes that we have already taken a look at in this guidebook, you will be able to see them quite a bit. This is because the assignment operator is simply going to be an equal sign, where you will assign a value over to a variable throughout the code. These kinds of operators are used to assign several values to the variables. Let's check the different types of assignment operators.

Operator	Description of the operator	Example
Equal (=)	This operator will assign values from right side operand to left side operand.	c = a + b;
Add AND (+=)	This operator will add the right operand with left operand and assigns the sum to the left operand.	c += a ⍰ it is equivalent to c = c + a;

Subtract AND (-=)	This operator will subtract the right operand from the left operand and assigns the subtraction to the left operand.	c -= a ⟶ it is equivalent to c = c - a;
Multiply AND (*=)	This operator will multiply the right and left operand and assigns the multiplication to the left operand.	c = a ⟶ *it is equivalent to c = c a;*
Divide AND (/=)	This operator will divide the left operand with the right operand and assigns division to the left operand.	c = a ⟶ *it's equivalent to c = ca;*
Modulus AND (%=)	This operator takes modulus by using both sides' operand and assigns the outcome to left operand.	c %= a ⟶ *it's equivalent to c = c % a;*
Exponent AND (**=)	Does 'to the power' calculation and assigns the outcome to the left operand.	c **= a ⟶ *it's equivalent to c = c**a*
Floor division AND (//=)	It does floor division and assigns the outcome to the left operand.	c //= a ⟶ *it's equivalent to c = c // a;*

So, if you are looking to assign the number 100 over to one of your variables, you would just need to put the equal sign there between them. This can be used with any kind of variable and value that you are using in your code, and you should already have some familiarity with getting this done ahead of time. It is also possible for you to go through and take several values, assigning them to the same variable if that is best for your code. As long as you have this assignment operator, or the equal sign, in between it, you will be able to add in as many values over to the variable that you would like.

Working with these operators is a simple thing to work with, but you will find that they show up in your coding regularly. You can use them to add your variables together, to use other mathematical operators, to assign a value over to the variable, or even a few values to your same variable. And you can even take these operators to compare two or more parts of the code at the same time and see if they are the same or not. As we can already see, there are so many things that we will be able to do when it comes to using these operators.

CHAPTER 6:

CLASSES

Definition of a Class

The keyword def is used to define a class in Python. The first string in a Python class is used to describe the class even though it is not always needed.

Example

Start IDLE.

Navigate to the File menu and click New Window.

Type the following:

class Dog

'''Briefly taking about class Dog using this docstring'''

Pass

Example 2

Start IDLE.

Navigate to the File menu and click New Window.

Type the following:

Class Bright:

"My other class"

b=10

def salute(self):

print('Welcome')

print(Bright.b)

print(Bright.salute)

print(Bright._doc_)

Classes and Objects in Python

Python supports different programming approaches as it is a multi-paradigm.

An object in Python has an attribute and behavior.

It is essential to understand objects and classes when studying machine learning using Python object-oriented programming language.

Example

Car as an object:

Attributes: color, mileage, model, age Behavior: reverse, speed, turn, roll, stop, start.

Class

It is a template for creating an object.

Example

class Car:

Note

By convention, we write the class name with the first letter as uppercase.

A class name is in singular form by convention.

Syntax

class Name_of_Class:

From a class, we can construct objects by simply making an instance of the class. The class_name() operator creates an object by assigning the object to the empty method.

Class or Object Instantiation

From our class Car, we can have several objects such as a first car, second care, or SUVs.

Example

Start IDLE.

Navigate to the File menu and click New Window.

Type the following:

my_car=Car()

 pass

Assignment

a. Create a class and an object for students.

b. Create a class and an object for the hospital.

c. Create a class and an object for a bank.

d. Create a class and an object for a police department.

Example

Start IDLE.

Navigate to the File menu and click New Window.

Type the following:

class Car:

category="Personal Automobile"

def _init_(self, model, insurance): self.model = model self.insurance =insurance   subaru=Car("Subaru","Insured") toyota=Car("Toyota","Uninsured")   print("Subaru is a {}".format(subaru._class_.car))   print("Toyota is a {}".format(toyota._class_.car))   print("{} is {}".format(subaru.model, subaru.insurance)) print("{} is {}".format(toyota.model, toyota.insurance))

Data Encapsulation/Data Hiding

Encapsulation in Python Object Oriented Programming approach is meant to help prevent data from direct modification. Private attributes in Python are denoted using a single or double underscore as a prefix.

Example

Start IDLE.

Navigate to the File menu and click New Window.

Type the following:

"__" or "_".

class Tv:

def _init_(self): self.__Finalprice = 800

def offer(self): print("Offering Price: {}".format(self.__finalprice))
def set_final_price(self, offer): self.__finalprice = offer t = Tv()

t.offer()

t.__finalprice = 950

t.offer()

using setter function

t.setFinalPrice(990)

t.sell()

Explanation

The program defined a class Tv and used *init(0* methods to hold the final offering price of the TV. Along the way, we attempted to change the price but could not manage. The reason for the inability to change is because Python treated the _finalprice as private attributes.

The only way to modify this value was through using a setter function, setMaxPrice() that takes price as a parameter.

Polymorphism

In Python, polymorphism refers to the ability to use a shared interface for several data types.

Start IDLE.

Navigate to the File menu and click New Window.

Type the following:

Explanation

The program above has defined two classes Tilapia and Shark all of which share the method jump() even though they have different functions.

By creating a common interface jumping_test() we allowed polymorphism in the program above.

We then passed objects bonny and biggie in the jumping_test() function.

Assignment

a. In a doctor consultation room suggest the class and objects in a programming context.

b. In a football team, suggest programming classes and objects.

c. In a grocery store, suggest programming classes and objects.

Creating an Object in Python

Example from the previous class Open the previous program file with class Bright student1=Bright()

Explanation

The last program will create object student1, a new instance. The attributes of objects can be accessed via the specific object name prefix. The attributes can be a method or data including the matching class functions. In other terms, Bright.salute is a function object and student1.salute will be a method object.

Example

Start IDLE.

Navigate to the File menu and click New Window.

Type the following:

class Bright:

"Another class again!"

c = 20

def salute(self): print('Hello') student2 = Bright()

print(Bright.salute)

print(student2.salute)

student2.salute()

Explanation

You invoked the student2.salute() despite the parameter 'self' and it still worked without placing arguments. The reason for this phenomenon is because each time an object calls its method, the object itself is passed as the first argument. The implication is that student2.salute() translates into student2.salute(student2). It is the reason for the 'self; name.

Constructors

Start IDLE.

Navigate to the File menu and click New Window.

Type the following:

class NumberComplex

class ComplexNumber:

def _init_(self,realnum = 0,i = 0): self.real = realnum self.imaginarynum = i def getData(self): print("{0}+{1}j".format(self.realnumber,self.imaginarynum)) complex1 = NumberComplex(2,3) complex1.getData()

complex2 = NumberComplex(5) complex2.attribute = 10

print((complex2.realnumber, complex2.imaginarynumber, complex2.attribute)) complex1.attribute

Deleting Objects and Attributes

The del statement is used to delete attributes of an object at any instance.

Example

Start IDLE.

Navigate to the File menu and click New Window.

Type the following:

complex1 = NumberComplex(2,3) del complex1.imaginarynumber complex1.getData()

del NumberComplex.getData

complex1.getData()

Deleting an Object

Example

Start IDLE.

Navigate to the File menu and click New Window.

Type the following:

complex1=NumberComplex(1,3) del complex1

Explanation

When complex1=NumberComplex(1,3) is done, a new instance of the object gets generated in memory, and the name complex1 ties with it.

The object does not immediately get destroyed as it temporarily stays in memory before the garbage collector purges it from memory.

The purging of the object helps free resources bound to the object and enhances system efficiency.

Garbage destruction Python refers to the automatic destruction of unreferenced objects.

Inheritance in Python

In Python inheritance allows us to specify a class that takes all the functionality from the base class and adds more. It is a powerful feature of OOP.

Syntax

class ParentClass:

 Body of parent class

class ChildClass(ParentClass): Body of derived class

Example

Start IDLE.

Navigate to the File menu and click New Window.

Type the following:

class Rect_mine(Rect_mine): def _init_(self): Shape._init_(self,4) def getArea(self): s1, s2, s3,s4 = self.count_sides perimeter = (s1+s2+s3+s4) area = (s1*s2) print('The rectangle area is:' %area)

Example 2

r = rect_mine()

r.inputSides()

Type b1 : 4

Type l1 : 8

Type b2 : 4

Type l1: 8

r.dispSides()

Type b1 is 4.0

Type l1 is 8.0

Type b2 is 4.0

Type l1 is 8.0

r.getArea()

Inheritance in Multiple Form

Example

Start IDLE. Navigate to the File menu and click New Window.

Type the following:

MultiInherit is derived from class Parent1 and Parent2.

Multilevel Inheritance

Inheriting from a derived class is called multilevel inheritance.

Example

Start IDLE.

Navigate to the File menu and click New Window.

Type the following:

class Parent:

 pass

class Multilevel1(Parent): pass

class Multilevel2(Multilevel1): pass

Explanation

Multilevel1 derives from Parent, and Multilevel2 derives from Multilevel1.

Method Resolution Order

Example

Start IDLE. Navigate to the File menu and click New Window.

Type the following:

print(issubclass(list,object))   print(isinstance(6.7,object))
print(isinstance("Welcome",object)) ***Explanation***

The specific attribute in a class will be scanned first.

The search will continue into parent classes.

This search does not repeat searching for the same class twice.

The approach or order of searching is sometimes called linearization of multi derived classes in Python.

The Method Resolution Order refers to the rules needed to determine this order.

Operator + Overloading

The *add()* function addition in a class will overload the +.

Example

Start IDLE.

Navigate to the File menu and click New Window.

Type the following:

```
class Planar:

    def _init_(self, x_axis= 0, y_axis = 0): self.x_axis = x_axis
    self.y_axis    =    y_axis    def    _str_(self):    return
    "({0},{1})".format(self.x_axis,self.y_axis) def _add_(self,z): x_axis
    = self.x_axis + z.x_axis y_axis = self.y_axis + z.y_axis return
    Planar(x_axis,y_axis)
```

Assignment

a. Print planar1 + planar2 from the example above.

Explanation

When you perform planar1+planar2 in Python, it will call planar.*add*(planar2) and in turn Planar.*add*(planar1, planar2).

Revisit Logical and Comparison Operators

Assignment

a. Given x=8, y=9, write a Python program that uses logical equals to test if x is equal to y.

b. Write a program that evaluates x!=y in Python programming language.

c. Write and run the following program m = True

n = False

print('m and n is',m and n) print('m or n is',m or n)

124

print('not m is',not n)

d. From the program in c., which program statement(s) evaluates to True, or False.

e. Write and run the following program in Python m1 = 15

n1 = 15

m2 = 'Welcome'

n2 = 'Welcome'

m3 = [11,12,13]

n3 = [11,12,13]

print(m1 is not n1)

print(m2 is n2)

print(m3 is n3)

f. Which program statement(s) generate True or False states in e.

g. Write and run the following program m = 'Welcome'

n = {11:'b',12:'c'}

print('W' in m)

print('Welcome' not in m)

print(10 in n)

print('b' in n)

h. Which program statement(s) in g. return True or False states.

The special functions needed for overloading other operators are listed below.

Overloading Comparison Operators

In Python, comparison operators can be overloaded.

Example

Assignment

a. Perform the following to the example above Planar(1,1)

b. Again perform Planar(1,1) in the above example.

c. Finally, perform Planar(1,1) from the above example.

Dictionaries

Dictionaries are data types in the Python programming language that is much similar to a list of certain objects contained in a particular collection. Let us venture into some of the similar characteristics and differences that lists and dictionaries share, so as to get the basic idea of what dictionaries are all about. Similar characteristics of these two data types include: They are both mutable, hence due to any shifting at any particular moment of time, they are dynamic. They are able to change in a way that they are to grow and shrink during any episodes and a dictionary is capable of containing another dictionary in it, and a list is too able to contain another list in it hence concluding that these data types can be nested. The only difference between these two data types comes from how the data values are accessed. Lists are normally accessed by various indexing operations whereas dictionaries are basically accessed by the use of various kinds of keys.

Dictionaries basically consist of some key-value pairs that normally are the key to a specified associated value. We define a dictionary in Python by first enclosing the entire list using curly brackets, placing a full colon that separates the key pairs to the associated value placed, and lastly by using a comma mark in separating the various kinds of key pairs that are available in the dictionary. Another way in which dictionaries can be constructed in the Python world is through the use of dict() function in the program. This one works in a way that the value of the argument in the dict() function consists of the keys and the respective values that have been paired along with it. Kindly remember that square brackets are normally used to contain the key-value pairs in the program in question. Once dictionaries have been defined, it is possible to display its contents where they get displayed just the same way they were defined structurally.

Dictionaries are accessed by specifying its relevant key inside square brackets symbol, and in a case where a certain key does not exist in a particular dictionary, an exception is raised right away as an error made. It is then possible to add a certain entry in a particular dictionary where a new key with its value is assigned in the program. In updating a particular entry, a new value is just assigned to an existing key. During the delete of an entry operation, a del statement is normally used specifying the actual key to delete.

Lastly, methods and various operations are normally implemented in dictionaries so various tasks can be achieved. For example, if a developer has the intention of copying a particular dictionary, he or she is obligated to use the copy() method of the Python programming language.

Some of the other methods include:

Clear method

This method clears all the kinds of elements that are present in the dictionary.

Get method

This one gives the value of the key that has been specified in the dictionary.

From keys

This kind of method gives out a particular number of keys and values from the dictionary.

Keys

Output a list that entails the keys in the dictionary.

Pop

This method removes the elements with the specified keys.

Exercise

Create a Dictionary "Hortons" with items containing keys as "type", "size" and "price" with corresponding values as "cappuccino", "grande" and "4.99".

Then add a new item with the key as "syrup" and value as "hazelnut".

Use Your Discretion Here And Write Your Code First

Now, check your code against the correct code below:

Hortons = {

"type" : "cappuccino",

"size" : "grande",

"price" : 4.99

}

Hortons ["syrup"] = "hazelnut"

print (Hortons)

Output – {"type" : "cappuccino", "size" : "grande", "price" : 4.99, "syrup" : "hazelnut"}

Exercise

Create a Dictionary "Hortons" with items containing keys as "type", "size", and "price" with corresponding values as "cappuccino", "grande" and "4.99".

Then use a function to remove the last added item.

Use Your Discretion Here And Write Your Code First

Now, check your code against the correct code below:

Hortons = {

"type" : "cappuccino",

"size" : "grande",

"price" : 4.99

}

Hortons.popitem ( )

print (Hortons)

Output – {"type" : "cappuccino", "size" : "grande"}

Exercise

Create a Dictionary "Hortons" with the nested dictionary as listed below: Dictionary Name Key Value

Coffee01 name cappuccino

size venti

Coffee02 name frappe

size grande

Coffee03 name macchiato

size small

Use Your Discretion Here And Write Your Code First

Now, check your code against the correct code below:

Hortons = {

"coffee01" : {

"name" : "cappuccino",

"size" : "venti"

},

"coffee02" : {

"name" : "frappe",

"size" : "grande"

},

"coffee03" : {

"name" : "macchiato",

"size" : "small"

}

}

print (Hortons)

Output - {"coffee01" : { "name" : "cappuccino", "size" : "venti"}, "coffee02" : {"name" : "frappe", "size" : "grande"}, "coffee03" : {"name" : "macchiato", "size" : "small"}}

Exercise

Use the "dict ()" function to create a Dictionary "Hortons" with items containing keys as "type", "size" and "price" with corresponding values as "cappuccino", "grande" and "4.99".

Use Your Discretion Here And Write Your Code First

Now, check your code against the correct code below:

Hortons = dict (type = "cappuccino", size = "grande", price = 4.99}

print (Hortons)

Output – {"type" : "cappuccino", "size" : "grande", "price" : 4.99, "syrup" : "hazelnut"}

Handling Your Exceptions

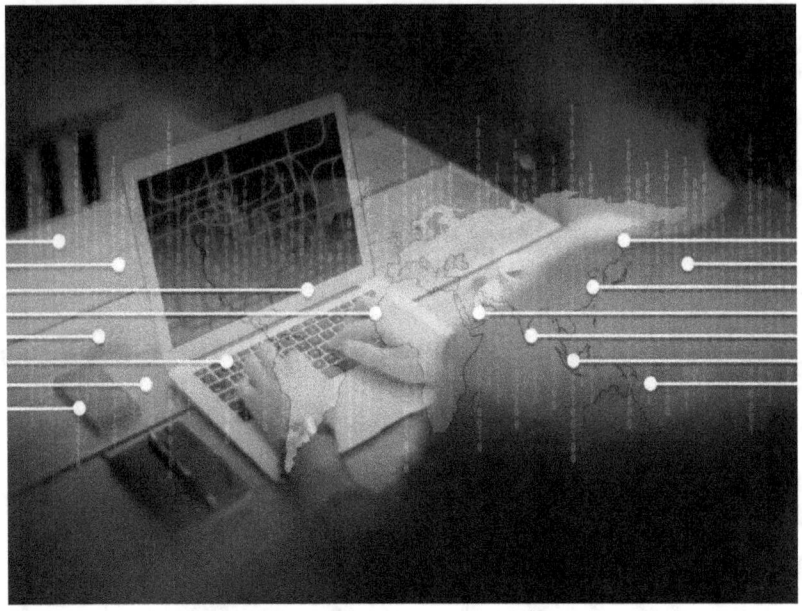

Another great thing that we can do when it comes to working with our Python language is known as exception handling. This is going to be a unique topic that we are going to spend a little bit of time on here because of its importance, but in the beginning, it is going to sound a little bit confusing. Don't worry though because you will catch on quickly, and it won't be long before you can raise an exception, make changes to the exception, and even create some of your exceptions that will be unique to the code that you are working with.

As you are going through some of the work that you need to handle in your code, you may find that there are going to be a few exceptions that the program is already going to bring out for you. And then there are also going to be a few that you will want to write on your own to ensure that the program is going to work the way that you would like. You will be able to find some of the automatic ones already in the standard library for Python. A good example of this is when you or the user will try to divide by zero in the code. The Python language will automatically not allow this to happen, so it is going to raise one of these exceptions for it. But if there is a special kind of exception that you want to work with when you are working on your codes, and you will be able to add this in as well. Now, the first part of this process is to raise an exception that the compiler will be able to recognize because of the standard library of Python. If the user does one of the things that will automatically bring it up the way that we want. This could be something simple like using an improper statement in our code or misspelling one of our classes so that the computer is not sure what you are looking for when you try to search for it at another time. These are things that the compiler is going to see as errors already, and you will need to go through and learn how to handle these. As a programmer, it is going to be your job, and a good idea, to know some of the kinds of exceptions that are going to be found in this kind of standard library with Python. This is going to be helpful to work with because it is going to tell us what to add into our codes, and when an exception is going to turn up for you.

How to Raise an Exception

The first thing that we are going to take a look at here is how to raise an exception inside of your code. We are going to work with some of the automatic ones that are going to show up. When you see these, you want to make sure that you are prepared and that you know what you can do to handle these and ensure that they are easier to work with and understand. If you are working on new code and you notice that there is a potential kind of issue that is showing up, or you want to go through the steps and figure out why your program is doing something that seems a bit off, then you may be able to check with the compiler and see that at this time, it is raising a new exception for you. This is because your program ran a bit, had a chance to take a look through the code, and found that it was not able to proceed. You then have to go through and check it out to figure out what is wrong and how you can fix this kind of issue. The good thing to remember here is that many times the issues you are dealing with will be simple, and you will be able to fix them pretty easily. For example, if you are going through your code and trying to bring up a file, and you provided it with the wrong name, either when you first named it or when it was time to call it up, your compiler is going to go through and raise a new exception. The program took the time to look through your code and noticed that there was stuff going on that it was not able to help you out with at all, and so it raised this exception. A good way for you to get into some of these exceptions and see how they work is to take some time to write out your examples and get some practice with them. This helps us to see what is going to happen when the compiler can raise one of the exceptions.

The code that you can use to see what happens with your compiler when you do it is going to be below:

x = 10

y = 10

result = x/y #trying to divide by zero

print(result)

The output that you are going to get when you try to get the interpreter to go through this code would be:

>>>

Traceback (most recent call last):

File "D: \Python34\tt.py", line 3, in <module>

result = x/y

ZeroDivisionError: division by zero

>>>

The picture above is going to be a good example of what is going to show up when we try to divide by zero. We can change up the message to make it work with what we should see within the code.

When you take a look at this example, your compiler is going to bring up an error, simply because you or the user is trying to divide by zero. This is not allowed with the Python code so it will raise that error. Now, if you leave it this way and you run the program exactly how it is, you are going to get a messy error message showing up, something that your user probably won't be able to understand. It makes the code hard to understand, and no one will know what to do next. A better idea is to look at some of the different options that you can add to your code to help prevent some of the mess from before. You want to make sure that the user understands why this exception is being raised, rather than leaving them confused in the process. A different way that you can write out this code to make sure that everyone is on the same page includes:

x = 10

y = 0

result = 0

try:

result = x/y

print(result)

except ZeroDivisionError:

print("You are trying to divide by zero.")

As you can see, the code that we just put into the compiler is going to be pretty similar to the one that we wrote above. But we did go through and change up the message to show something unless the user raises this exception. When they do get this exception, they will see the message "You are trying to divide by zero" come up on the screen. This isn't a necessary step, but it definitely makes your code easier to use!

How to Define My Exceptions

The next thing that we need to take a look at is some of the steps that we can use to raise our exceptions. With the work that we did above, we spent our time handling any of the automatic exceptions that were found by the program and that the standard library of Python was going to recognize. Then we went a bit further and found out some of the steps that we can use to personalize the message that comes with that exception, rather than just leaving it automatically that most non-programmers, or your regular users, are not going to understand.

Now that we have that out of the way, it is time for us to take our exception writing skills to the next level, and learn how we can write some of our exceptions to fit the kinds of codes that we are writing. This is not going to come into play all of the time, but sometimes it can be helpful to make sure you are going to get everything done the way that you would like.

For example, maybe you are working on some new program or code, and you want to set it up so that your users are only going to be able to add in the input of certain numbers, and then not allow some of the other numbers. Or you could have an exception that will show up when the user tries to guess more than three times. These are both things that could come up in a game, and having the process set up to handle these, and raising some of your exceptions can make a big difference.

Keep in mind with some of these kinds of exceptions that they are unique to the program that you are creating. If you don't specifically add these exceptions into the mix, then the compiler won't recognize that there is anything wrong here, and will just keep going. You can add in as many of these exceptions, and any kind of exception that you would like, and it is going to follow a fairly similar idea to what we say before. The code that we are going to use to ensure that this happens the way that we want though will include:

class CustomException(Exception):

def_init_(self, value):

self.parameter = value

def_str_(self):

return repr(self.parameter)

try:

raise CustomException("This is a CustomError!")

except for CustomException as ex:

print("Caught:", ex.parameter)

When you finish this particular code, you are done successfully adding in your exception. When someone does raise this exception, the message "Caught: This is a CustomError!" will come up on the screen. You can always change the message to show whatever you would like, but this was there as a placeholder to show what we are doing. Take a moment here to add this to the compiler and see what happens.

There are a lot of different times when you will want to work with exception handling. This is something that we are going to focus on more and more when we bring in some of the advanced types of codes that are possible with Python. There are many times that you can work with both types of exceptions that were discussed in this chapter, and you will find that they are going to help you to get more done overall. Make sure to practice some of the codes above to make sure that you have exception handling down and ready to go.

CONCLUSION

Even though this is the end of this book, I sincerely hope that it is just the beginning of your Python journey. Python has been growing steadily in popularity over the last decade and is increasingly used in all areas of computing. You will find Python powering popular websites such as Pinterest, Instagram, and Reddit. Python is used in scientific computing and is running on supercomputers around the world. It's used for system administration tasks like configuration and package management with YUM and anaconda being prime examples.

Every measure was taken into consideration to ensure that all the chapters give you detailed and easy to understand information. I intentionally used simple language throughout the book to make sure that you get empowered after reading. The book has deliberately avoided sophisticated theories and stuck to simple Explanations that you can use at your convenience when studying.

The thing about computer programming is that your learning will never stop. Even if you think that you have the basics down pat if you don't use what you have learned regularly, believe me when I say that you will soon forget it! Computer programming is evolving on an almost daily basis and it's up to you to keep up with everything that is going on. To that end, you would be well advised to join a few of the Python communities. You will find many of these on the internet and they are places where you can stay up to the minute with changes, where you can join in conversations, discuss code, and ask for help. Eventually, you will be in a position of being able to help the newbies on the scene and it is then that you will realize just how far you have come. So, where do you go from here? The first thing to do is go over this book as many times as necessary to let the content sink in. Don't just read it once and think that you know it all because you don't. The human brain can only take in so much information in one go and it needs time to assimilate that information and store it away before the next influx. Trying to take in pages and pages of code and information will not serve you well and it isn't a case of being the quickest to read it. You can read as much as you like but, once your brain stops taking information in, anything else will be meaningless.

Take your time; do the exercises as many times as you need to until you know that you can write the answers AND understand the answers in your sleep. That is important – it is not enough to know the answers with Python programming. You have to be able to understand WHY the answer is such, the process that gets to that answer if you don't understand the code from start to finish you will never be able to understand the answers.

I hope this book was able to help you to learn the fundamentals of Python Programming quickly and easily and inspire you to create your meaningful programs and practical applications.

The power of programming languages in our digital world cannot be underestimated. People are increasingly reliant on the modern conveniences of smart technology and that momentum will endure for a long time. With all the instructions provided in this book, you are now ready to start developing your own innovative smart tech ideas and turn it into a major tech startup company and guide mankind towards a smarter future.

It is important not to feel like heroes when a program works but above all you should not be depressed when you cannot find a solution to your programming problems. The network is full of sites and blogs where you can always find a solution.

Make it your routine to combine some practical sessions to improve your python programming skills. If you are working with an experienced programmer, follow all the instructions provided to you, and ask questions where you do not understand.

Do whatever you have identified as necessary to improve applications of programming in real life. You will realize that the majority of those who seem to have it all together lack the basic Python programming skills. Try to engage them and teach them a thing or two you have learned herein. You may even recommend or give this book to them.

Good luck.

www.ingramcontent.com/pod-product-compliance
Lightning Source LLC
LaVergne TN
LVHW011714060526
838200LV00051B/2900